CELTIC CHARTED DESIGNS

by Co Spinhoven

DOVER PUBLICATIONS, INC. · NEW YORK

To my friends Alan and Joan Ginsberg
in Bethel, Gwynedd, for drawing my attention to
the beauty of Celtic art.

Copyright © 1987 by Co Spinhoven.
All rights reserved under Pan American and International
Copyright Conventions.

Published in Canada by General Publishing Company, Ltd.,
30 Lesmill Road, Don Mills, Toronto, Ontario.
Published in the United Kingdom by Constable and Company, Ltd.

Celtic Charted Designs is a new work, first published
by Dover Publications, Inc., in 1987.

Manufactured in the United States of America
Dover Publications, Inc.
31 East 2nd Street
Mineola, N.Y. 11501

Library of Congress Cataloging-in-Publication Data

Spinhoven, Co
Celtic charted designs.

1. Needlework—Patterns. 2. Decoration and ornament,
Celtic. I. Title.
TT753.S65   1987   746.4   87-9098
ISBN 0-486-25411-9 (pbk.)

Introduction

The distinctive spirals and elaborate knotwork so characteristic of Celtic design can be found on pieces made using a wide variety of techniques. Stonework such as the Crosses of Moone and Muiredach, metalwork such as the Petrie Crown and the Ardagh Chalice, jewelry such as the Tara Brooch, and, of course, magnificent illuminated manuscripts such as the Books of Kells and Durrow and the Lindisfarne Gospels, are all examples of the enduring beauty of Celtic art. Today, Celtic motifs are extremely popular for a number of different crafts from jewelry making to embroidery to quilting.

Celtic designs are often extremely elaborate and highly structured. The methods used to construct them are imperfectly understood, although many attempts to duplicate them have been made. This book is partly a visual method of constructing such designs in charted form, but even more it is a rich collection of charts for immediate use. Using these charts, Celtic motifs can be used to create beautiful cross-stitch pictures, needlepoint pillows, latchhook rugs, knitted or crocheted garments, woven fabrics and much, much more. General instructions for a number of popular charted techniques are given below.

The charts include designs drawn from authentic Celtic sources, a few designs from other cultures that are extremely similar to Celtic designs, original designs and designs meant to illustrate the construction of, and the relationship between, various elements in Celtic art. The early plates do not show specific Celtic designs at all, but instead, explore various basic arrangements of black-and-white squares. Design #1 on Plate 1 shows the most elementary division of black and white that can be made; design #2 illustrates the result of reversing the color of every 3rd square of every 3rd row; design #3 is an expanded version of #2 and so on. The numbers printed in the arrows on the pages indicate the number of the design, but the direction of the arrows indicates the relationship between the designs—#1 leading to #2 and #6; #2 leading to #3; #3 leading to #4; etc.

The designs have been divided into four groups:

1. Step, fret and key patterns (Plates 1–17)—rectangular and straight forms;
2. Spiral work (Plates 18–31)—round and curved forms;
3. Knotwork (Plates 32–50)—interlaced forms;
4. Biomorphic ornaments (Plates 51–57)—representations of plants, animals and people.

The charts in the first three groups begin with the simplest, most basic designs, then move on to more complex designs.

Colors are not indicated on the charts because the structure of the design is more easily seen if the design is reduced to its simplest form. Occasionally a third color is introduced where finer detail is needed.

On several of the plates are charts that illustrate details of the construction of a design. For example, the first few charts on Plates 18 and 19 show how a rectangular pattern can be transformed into a spiral. Plate 25 shows the construction of a spiral panel from the Shandwick Stone in Ross-shire, Scotland. First the circle is divided into sixteen equal parts as shown by the gray guidelines. The three rings of spirals are then constructed between these guidelines. The actual panel that this design was taken from is a rectangle; the completion of the top half of the pattern is shown in gray and one complete corner is shown at the upper right of the page. Design #240 on Plate 32 shows the translation of a charted horizontal or vertical band into its diagonal equivalent. Design #243 on the same plate shows the framework for the interlaced design on Plate 31. In designs #304 and #306 on Plate 43, #319 on Plate 45 and #325 and #326 on Plate 46, the shaded area shows one complete unit of the design.

The eleven full-page charts are original designs, developed by combining various elements of Celtic art. Many of these designs are too large to fit completely on the page. At least one quarter or one half of the design is shown in full, with the center of the incomplete edges marked by a thick black line. To complete the design, reverse the pattern at the center.

COUNTED CROSS-STITCH

MATERIALS

1. **Needles.** A small blunt tapestry needle, No. 24 or No. 26.
2. **Fabric.** Evenweave linen, cotton, wool or synthetic fabrics all work well. The most popular fabrics are aida cloth, linen and hardanger cloth. Cotton aida is most commonly available in 18 threads-per-inch, 14 threads-per-inch and 11 threads-per-inch (14-count is the most popular size). Evenweave linen comes in a variety of threads-per-inch. To work cross-stitch on linen involves a slightly different technique (see page iv). Thirty thread-per-inch linen will result in a stitch about the same size as 14-count aida. Hardanger cloth has 22 threads to the inch and is available in cotton or linen. The amount of fabric needed depends on the size of the cross-stitch design. To determine yardage, divide the number of stitches in the design by the thread-count of the fabric. For example: If a design 112 squares wide by 140 squares deep is worked on a 14-count fabric, divide 112 by 14 (=8), and 140 by 14 (=10). The design will measure 8″ × 10″. The same design worked on 22-count fabric measures about 5″ × 6½″.
3. **Threads and Yarns.** Six-strand embroidery floss, crewel wool, Danish Flower Thread, pearl cotton or metallic threads all work well for cross-stitch. Crewel wool works well on

evenweave wool fabric. Danish Flower Thread is a thicker thread with a matte finish, one strand equaling two of embroidery floss.

4. **Embroidery Hoop.** A wooden or plastic 4″, 5″ or 6″ round or oval hoop with a screw-type tension adjuster works best for cross-stitch.

5. **Scissors.** A pair of sharp embroidery scissors is essential to all embroidery.

PREPARING TO WORK

To prevent raveling, either whip stitch or machine-stitch the outer edges of the fabric.

Locate the exact center of the chart. Establish the center of the fabric by folding it in half first vertically, then horizontally. The center stitch of the chart falls where the creases of the fabric meet. Mark the fabric center with a basting thread.

It is best to begin cross-stitch at the top of the design. To establish the top, count the squares up from the center of the chart, and the corresponding number of holes up from the center of the fabric.

Place the fabric tautly in the embroidery hoop, for tension makes it easier to push the needle through the holes without piercing the fibers. While working continue to retighten the fabric as necessary.

When working with multiple strands (such as embroidery floss) always separate (strand) the thread before beginning to stitch. This one small step allows for better coverage of the fabric. When you need more than one thread in the needle, use separate strands and do not double the thread. (For example: If you need four strands, use four separated strands.) Thread has a nap (just as fabrics do) and can be felt to be smoother in one direction than the other. Always work with the nap (the smooth side) pointing down.

For 14-count aida and 30-count linen, work with two strands of six-strand floss. For more texture, use more thread; for a flatter look, use less thread.

EMBROIDERY

To begin, fasten the thread with a waste knot and hold a short length of thread on the underside of the work, anchoring it with the first few stitches (*Diagram 1*). When the thread end is securely in place, clip the knot.

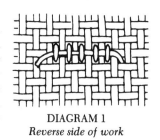

DIAGRAM 1
Reverse side of work

To stitch, push the needle up through a hole in the fabric, cross the thread intersection (or square) on a left-to-right diagonal (*Diagram 2*). Half the stitch is now completed.

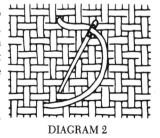

DIAGRAM 2

Next, cross back, right to left, forming an X (*Diagram 3*).

Work all the same color stitches on one row, then cross back, completing the X's (*Diagram 4*).

DIAGRAM 3   DIAGRAM 4

Some needleworkers prefer to cross each stitch as they come to it. This method also works, but be sure all of the top stitches are slanted in the same direction. Isolated stitches must be crossed as they are worked. Vertical stitches are crossed as shown in *Diagram 5*.

DIAGRAM 5

At the top, work horizontal rows of a single color, left to right. This method allows you to go from an unoccupied space to an occupied space (working from an empty hole to a filled one), making ruffling of the floss less likely. Holes are used more than once, and all stitches "hold hands" unless a space is indicated on the chart. Hold the work upright throughout (do not turn as with many needlepoint stitches).

When carrying the thread from one area to another, run the needle under a few stitches on the wrong side. Do not carry thread across an open expanse of fabric as it will be visible from the front when the project is completed.

To end a color, weave in and out of the underside of the stitches, making a scallop stitch or two for extra security (*Diagram 6*). When possible, end in the same direction in which you were working, jumping up a row if necessary (*Diagram 7*). This prevents holes caused by stitches being pulled in two directions. Trim the thread ends closely and do not leave any tails or knots as they will show through the fabric when the work is completed.

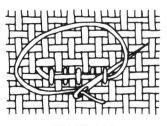

DIAGRAM 6
Reverse side of work

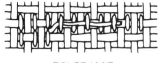

DIAGRAM 7
Reverse side of work

Embroidery on Linen. Working on linen requires a slightly different technique. While evenweave linen is remarkably regular, there are always a few thick or thin threads. To keep the stitches even, cross-stitch is worked over two threads in each direction (*Diagram 8*).

As you are working over more threads, linen affords a

DIAGRAM 8

DIAGRAM 9

greater variation in stitches. A half-stitch can slant in either direction and is uncrossed. A three-quarters stitch is shown in *Diagram 9*.

Embroidery on Gingham. Gingham and other checked fabrics can be used for cross-stitch. Using the fabric as a guide, work the stitches from corner to corner of each check.

Embroidery on Uneven-Weave Fabrics. If you wish to work cross-stitch on an uneven-weave fabric, baste a lightweight Penelope needlepoint canvas to the material. The design can then be stitched by working the cross-stitch over the double mesh of the canvas. When working in this manner, take care not to catch the threads of the canvas in the embroidery. After the cross-stitch is completed, remove the basting threads. With tweezers remove first the vertical threads, one strand at a time, of the needlepoint canvas, then the horizontal threads.

NEEDLEPOINT

One of the most common methods for working needlepoint is from a charted design. By simply viewing each square of a chart as a stitch on the canvas, the patterns quickly and easily translate from one technique to another.

MATERIALS

1. **Needles.** A blunt tapestry needle with a rounded tip and an elongated eye. The needle must clear the hole of the canvas without spreading the threads. For No. 10 canvas, a No. 18 needle works best.

2. **Canvas.** There are two distinct types of needlepoint canvas: single-mesh (mono canvas) and double-mesh (Penelope canvas). Single-mesh canvas, the more common of the two, is easier on the eyes as the spaces are slightly larger.

Double-mesh canvas has two horizontal and two vertical threads forming each mesh. The latter is a very stable canvas on which the threads stay securely in place as the work progresses. Canvas is available in many sizes, from 5 mesh-per-inch to 18 mesh-per-inch, and even smaller. The number of mesh-per-inch will, of course, determine the dimensions of the finished needlepoint project. A 60 square × 120 square chart will measure 12″ × 24″ on 5 mesh-to-the-inch canvas, 5″ × 10″ on 12 mesh-to-the-inch canvas. The most common canvas size is 10 to the inch.

3. **Yarns.** Persian, crewel and tapestry yarns all work well on needlepoint canvas.

PREPARING TO WORK

Allow 1″ to 1½″ blank canvas all around. Bind the raw edges of the canvas with masking tape or machine-stitched double-fold bias tape.

There are few hard-and-fast rules on where to begin the design. It is best to complete the main motif, then fill the background as the last step.

For any guidelines you wish to draw on the canvas, take care that your marking medium is waterproof. Nonsoluble inks, acrylic paints thinned with water so as not to clog the mesh, and waterproof felt-tip pens all work well. If unsure, experiment on a scrap of canvas.

When working with multiple strands (such as Persian yarn) always separate (strand) the yarn before beginning to stitch. This one small step allows for better coverage of the canvas. When you need more than one piece of yarn in the needle, use separate strands and do not double the yarn. For example: If you need two strands of 3-ply Persian yarn, use two separated strands. Yarn has a nap (just as fabrics do) and can be felt to be smoother in one direction than the other. Always work with the nap (the smooth side) pointing down.

For 5 mesh-to-the-inch canvas, use six strands of 3-ply yarn; for 10 mesh-to-the-inch canvas, use three strands of 3-ply yarn.

STITCHING

Cut yarn lengths 18″ long. Begin needlepoint by holding about 1″ of loose yarn on the wrong side of the work and working the first several stitches over the loose end to secure it. To end a piece of yarn, run it under several completed stitches on the wrong side of the work.

There are hundreds of needlepoint stitch variations, but tent stitch is universally considered to be *the* needlepoint stitch. The most familiar versions of tent stitch are half-cross stitch, continental stitch and basket-weave stitch.

Half-cross stitch (*Diagram 10*) is worked from left to right. The canvas is then turned around and the return row is again stitched from left to right. Holding the needle vertically, bring it to the front of the canvas through the hole that will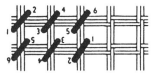

DIAGRAM 10

be the bottom of the first stitch. Keep the stitches loose for minimum distortion and good coverage. Half-cross stitch is best worked on a double-mesh canvas.

Continental stitch (*Diagram 11*) begins in the upper right-hand corner and is worked from right to left. The needle is slanted and always brought out a mesh ahead. The resulting stitch appears as a half-cross stitch on the front and as a slanting stitch on the back. When the row is complete, turn the canvas around to work the return row, continuing to stitch from right to left.

DIAGRAM 11

Basket-weave stitch (*Diagram 12*) begins in the upper right-hand corner with four continental stitches (two stitches worked horizontally across the top and two placed directly below the first stitch). Work diagonal rows, the first slanting up and across the canvas from right to left, and the next down and across from left to right. Moving down the canvas from left to right, the needle is in a vertical position; working in the opposite direction, the needle is horizontal. The rows interlock, creating a basket-weave pattern on the wrong side. If the stitch is not done properly, a faint ridge will show where the pattern was interrupted. On basket-weave stitch, always stop working in the middle of a row, rather than at the end, so that you will know in which direction you were working.

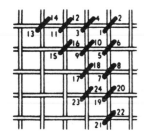

DIAGRAM 12

KNITTING

Charted designs can be worked into stockinette stitch as you are knitting, or they can be embroidered with duplicate stitch when the knitting is complete. For the former, wind the different colors of yarn on bobbins and work in the same manner as in Fair Isle knitting. A few quick Fair Isle tips: (1) Always bring up the new color yarn from under the dropped color to prevent holes. (2) Carry the color not in use loosely across the wrong side of the work, but not more than three or four stitches without twisting the yarns. If a color is not in use for more than seven or eight stitches, it is usually best to drop that color yarn and rejoin a new bobbin when the color is again needed.

CROCHET

There are a number of ways in which charts can be used for crochet. Among them are:

SINGLE CROCHET

Single crochet is often seen worked in multiple colors. When changing colors, always pick up the new color for the last yarn-over of the old color. The color not in use can be carried loosely across the back of the work for a few stitches, or you can work the single crochet over the unused color. The latter method makes for a neater appearance on the wrong side, but sometimes the old color peeks through the stitches. This method can also be applied to half-double crochet and double crochet, but keep in mind that the longer stitches will distort the design.

FILET CROCHET

This technique is nearly always worked from charts and uses only one color thread. The result is a solid-color piece with the design filled in and the background left as an open mesh. Care must be taken in selecting the design, as the longer stitch causes distortion.

AFGHAN CROCHET

The most common method here is cross-stitch worked over the afghan stitch. Complete the afghan crochet project. Then, following the chart for color placement, work cross-stitch over the squares of crochet.

OTHER CHARTED METHODS

Latch hook, Assisi embroidery, beading, cross-stitch on needlepoint canvas (a European favorite) and lace net embroidery are among the other needlework methods worked from charts.

PLATE 1

PLATE 2

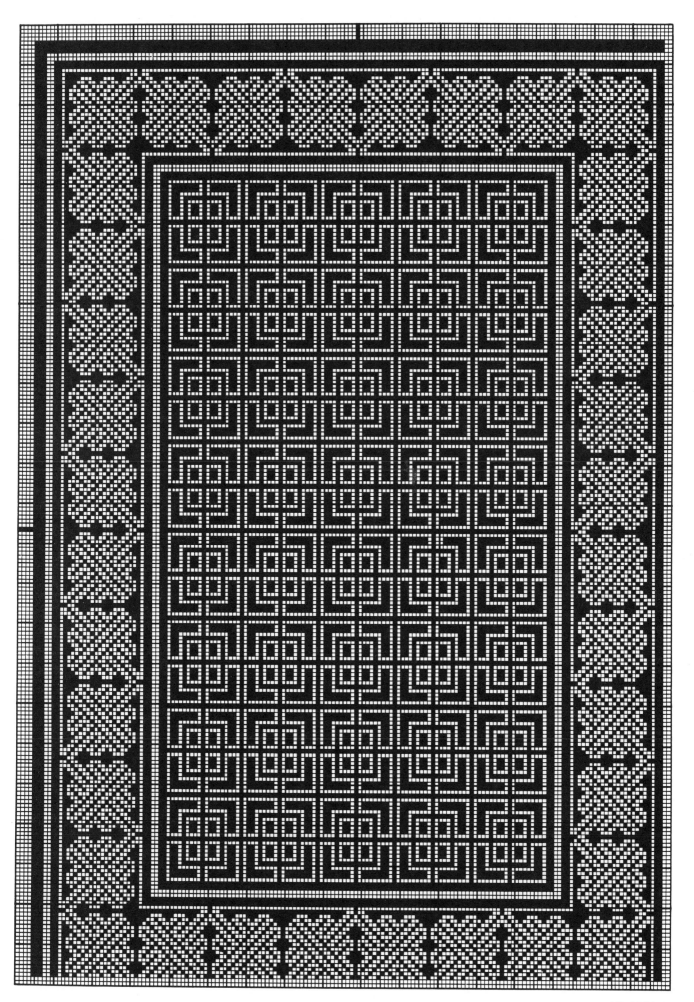

PLATE 3

PLATE 4

PLATE 5

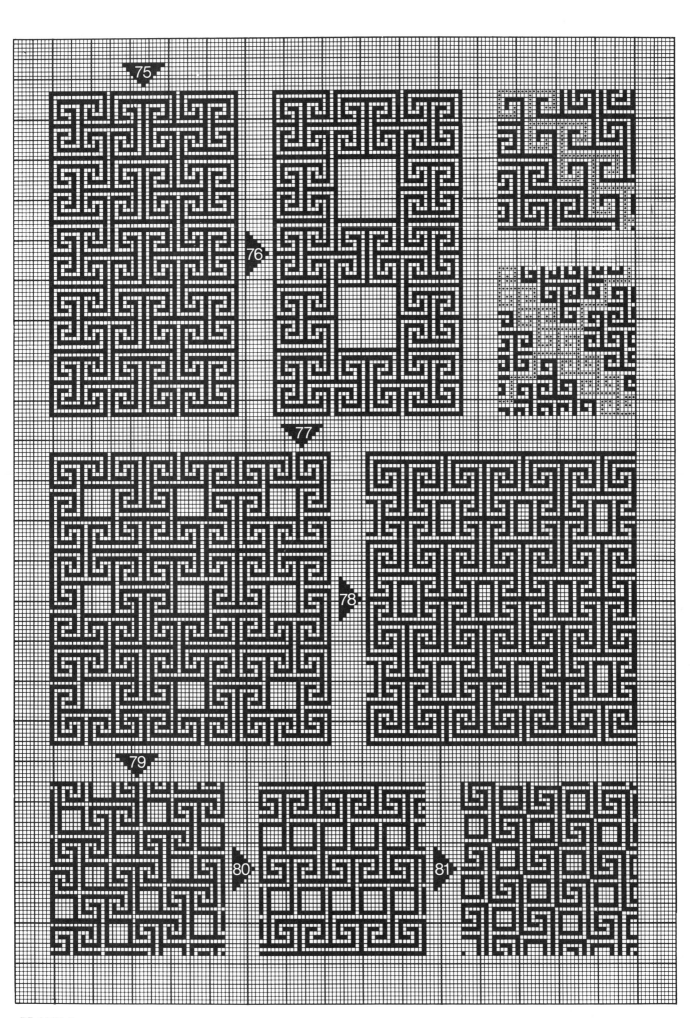

PLATE 6

PLATE 7

PLATE 8

PLATE 9

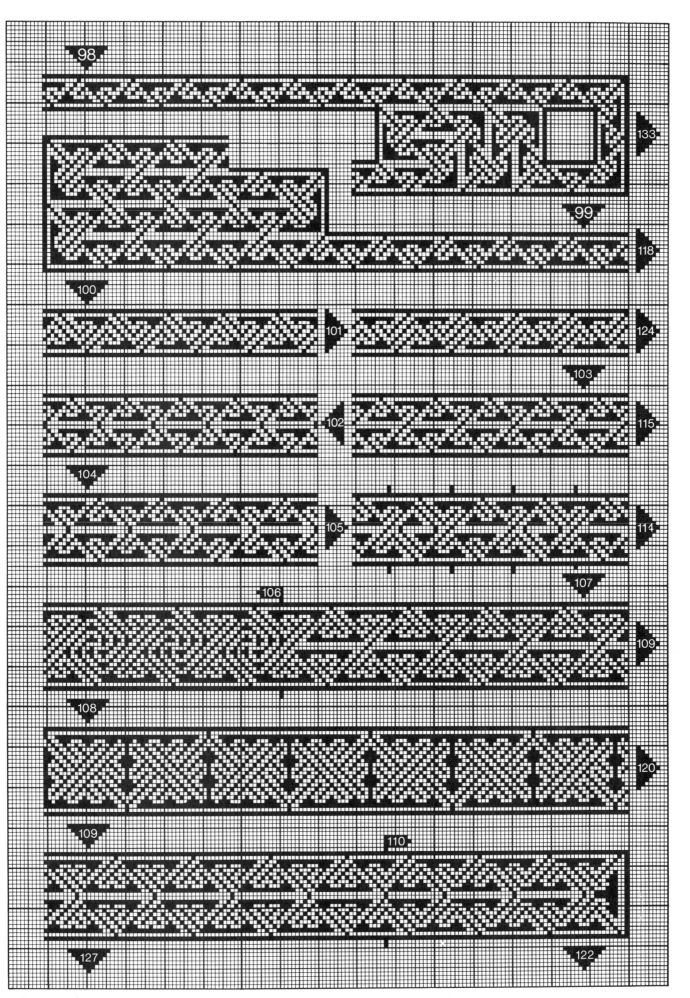

PLATE 10

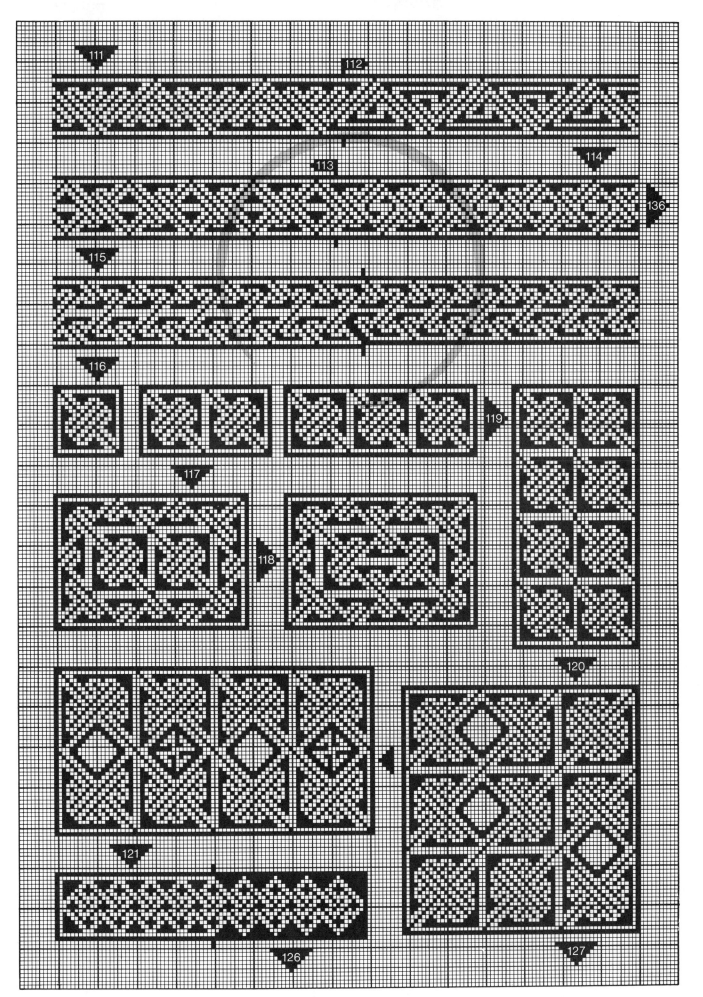

PLATE 11

PLATE 12

PLATE 13

PLATE 14

PLATE 15

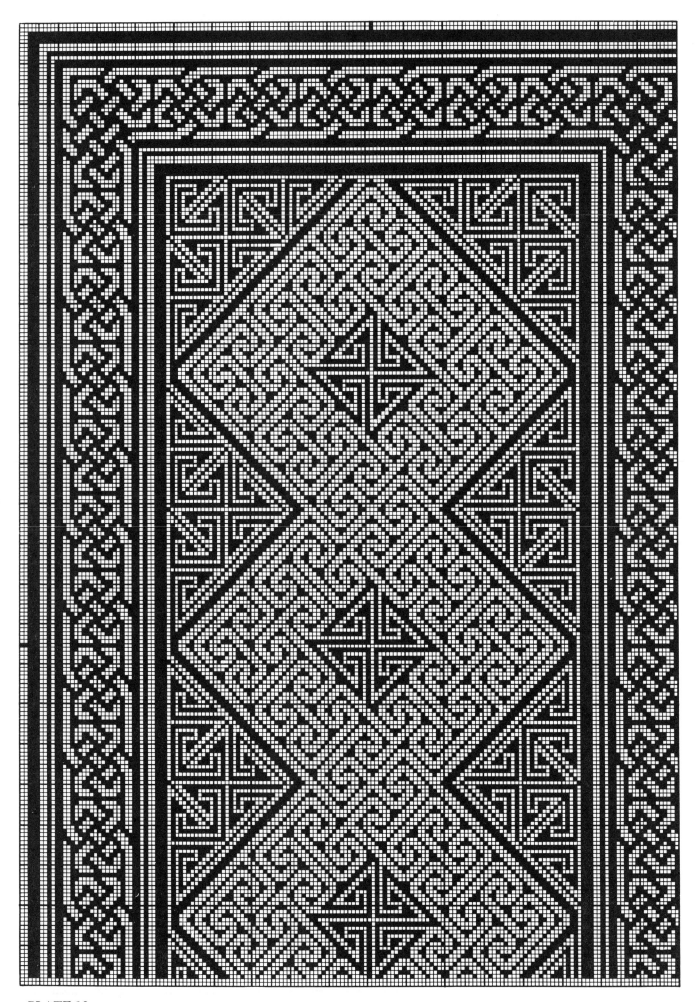

PLATE 16

PLATE 17

PLATE 18

PLATE 19

PLATE 20

PLATE 21

PLATE 22

PLATE 23

PLATE 24

220

221

PLATE 25

PLATE 26

PLATE 27

PLATE 28

PLATE 29

PLATE 30

PLATE 31

PLATE 32

PLATE 33

PLATE 34

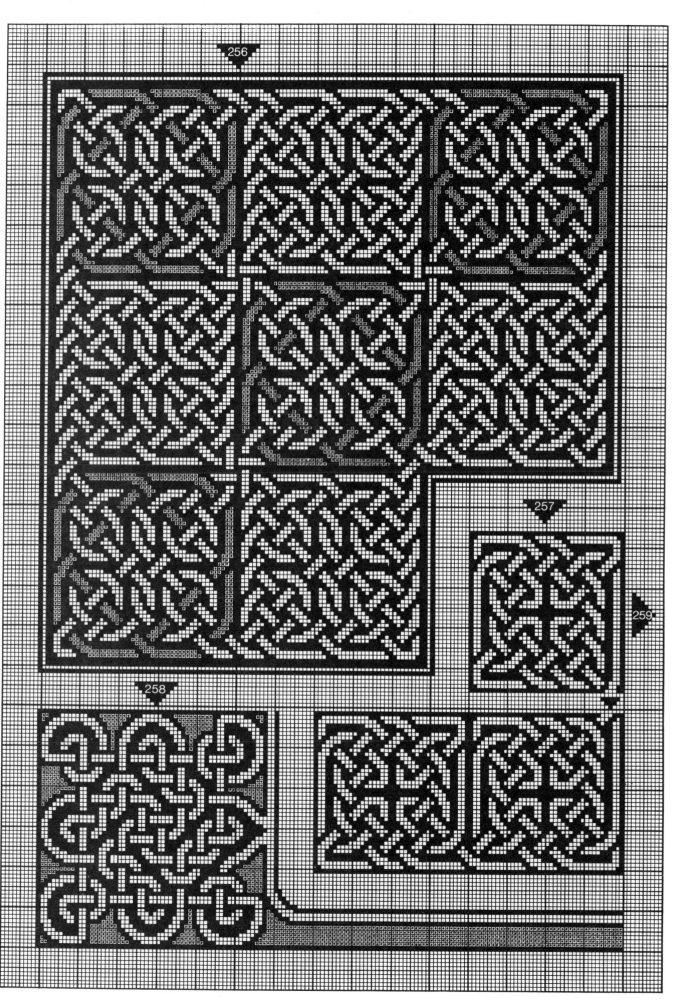

PLATE 35

PLATE 36

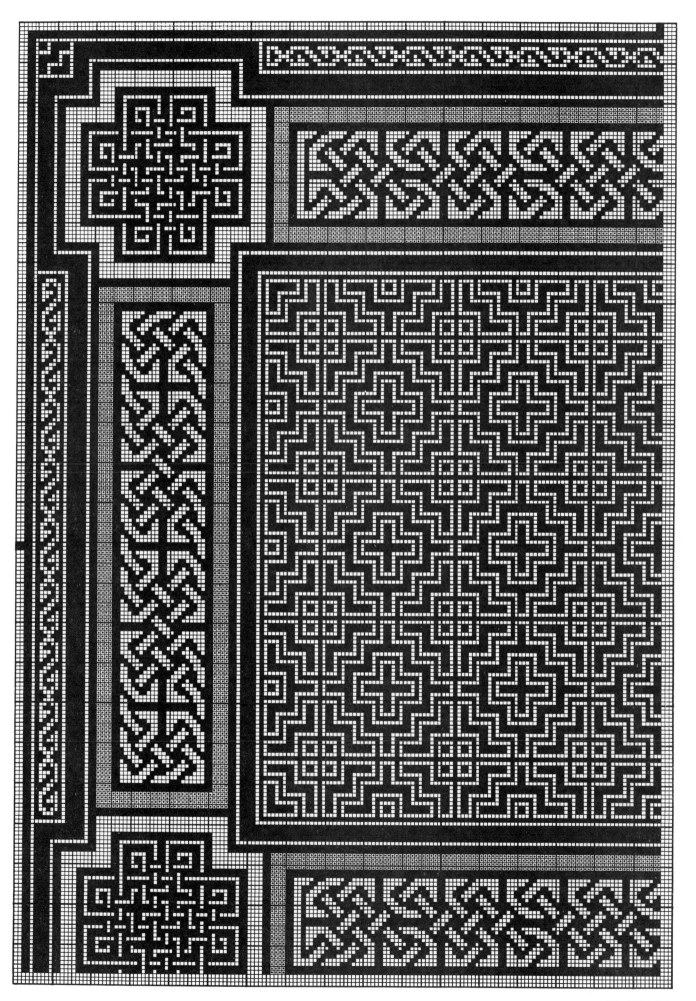

PLATE 37

PLATE 38

PLATE 39

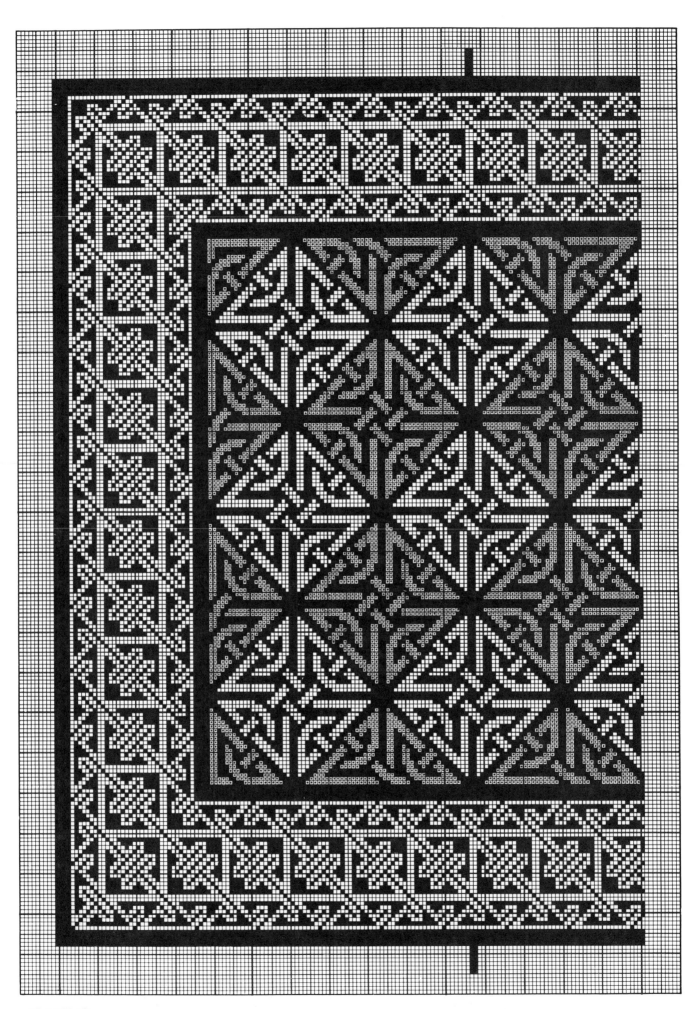

PLATE 40

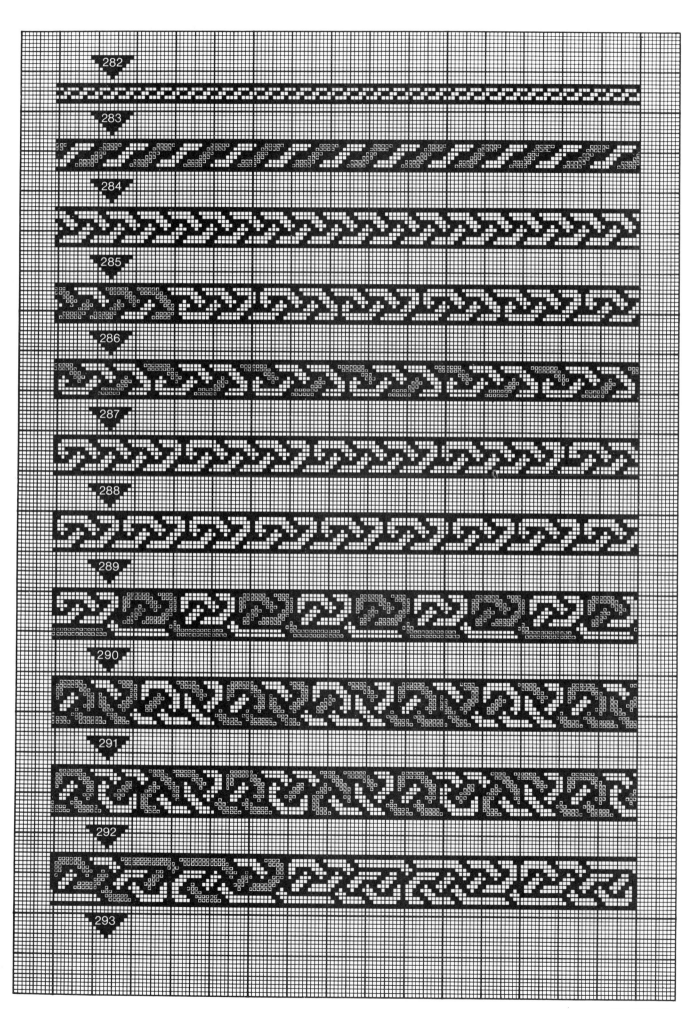

282

283

284

285

286

287

288

289

290

291

292

293

PLATE 41

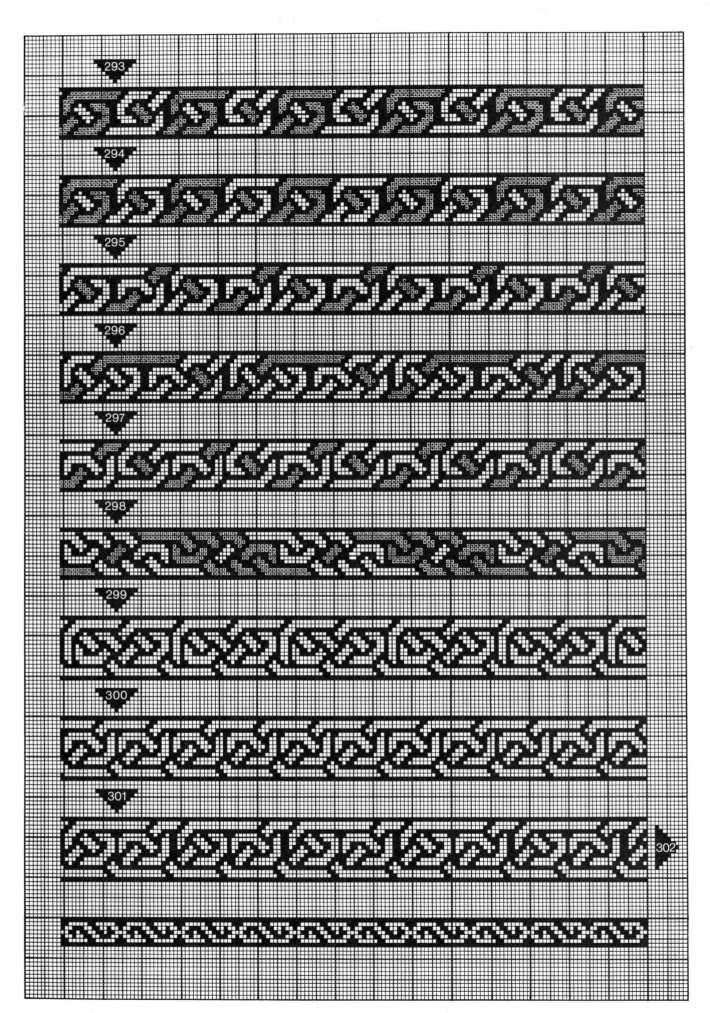

PLATE 42

302

303

304

305

306

307

308

309

310

PLATE 43

PLATE 44

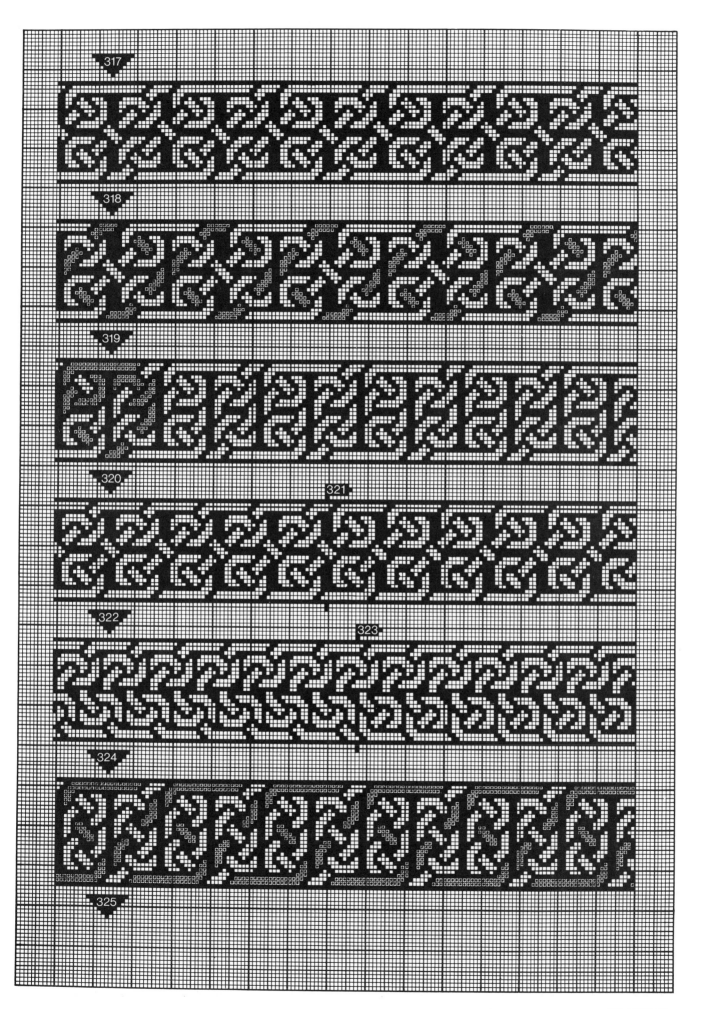

PLATE 45

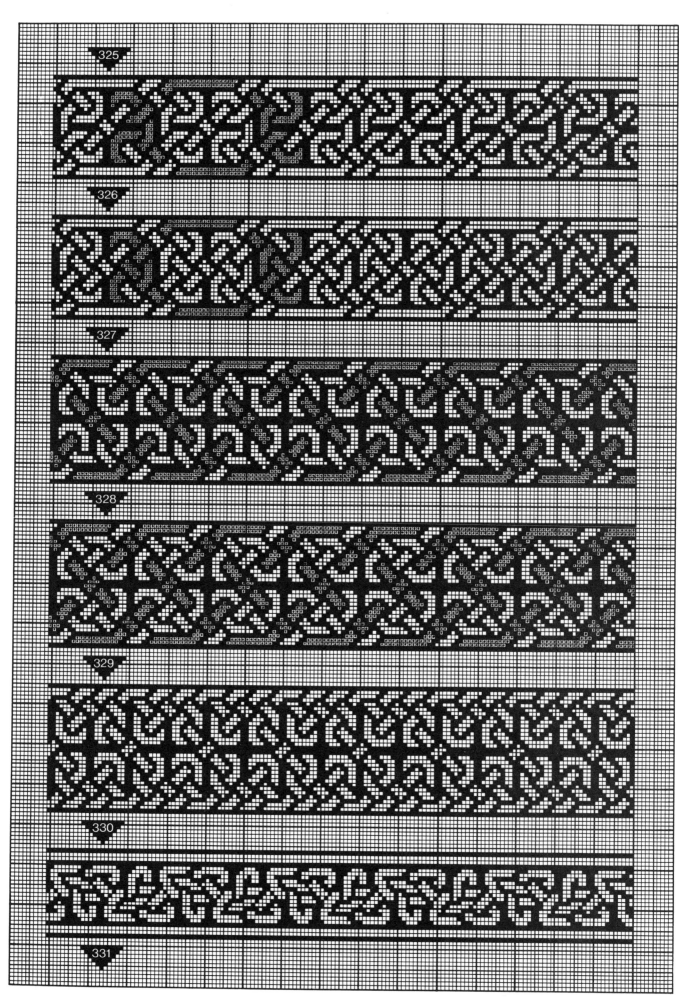

PLATE 46

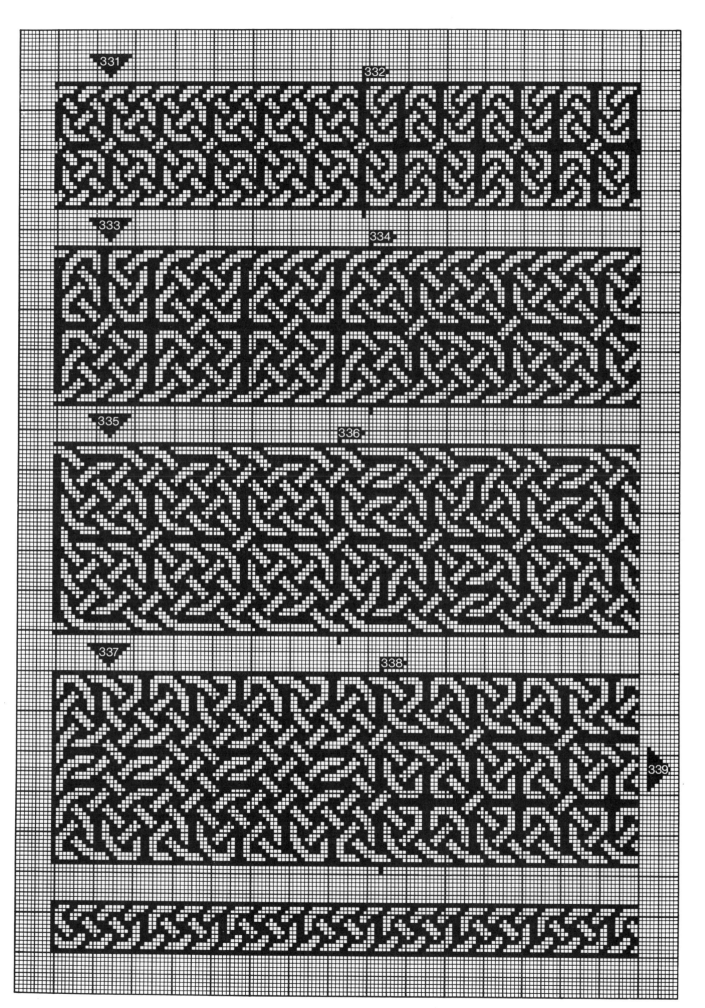

PLATE 47

PLATE 48

344

345

346

PLATE 49

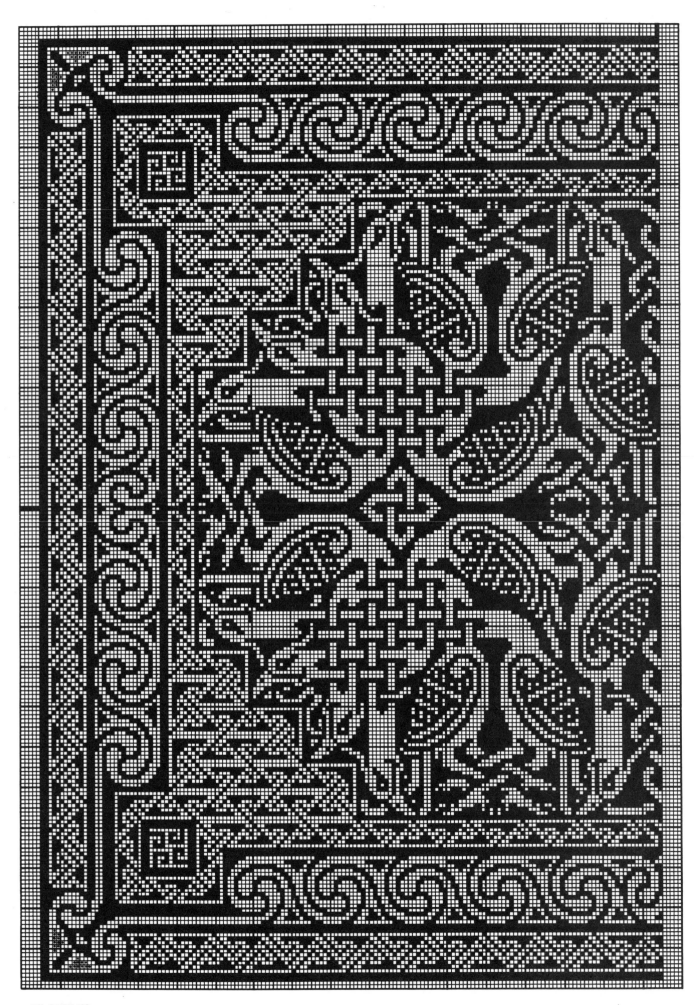

PLATE 50

PLATE 51

354

355

356

357

358

359

360

PLATE 52

PLATE 53

PLATE 54

PLATE 55

PLATE 56

PLATE 57